21st Century
Basic Skills
Library

PATTERNS IN FOOD

by Rebecca Felix

Cherry Lake Publishing • Ann Arbor, Michigan

2

Published in the United States of America
by Cherry Lake Publishing
Ann Arbor, Michigan
www.cherrylakepublishing.com

Consultants: Janice A. Bradley, PhD; Marla Conn, ReadAbility, Inc.

Editorial direction and book production: Red Line Editorial

Photo Credits: Purestock/Thinkstock, cover, 1; iStock/Thinkstock, 4; Matka Wariatka/Shutterstock Images, 6; Varina and Jay Patel/Shutterstock Images, 8; iStockphoto, 10, 16; Thomas Northcut/Photodisc/Thinkstock, 12; BananaStock/Thinkstock, 14; Dave & Les Jacobs/Blend Images/Thinkstock, 18; Joe Gough/Shutterstock Images, 20

Library of Congress Cataloging-in-Publication Data
Felix, Rebecca, 1984-
  Patterns in food / by Rebecca Felix.
      pages cm. -- (Patterns all around)
  Includes index.
  ISBN 978-1-63188-920-2 (hardcover : alk. paper) -- ISBN 978-1-63188-936-3 (pbk. : alk. paper) -- ISBN 978-1-63188-952-3 (pdf) -- ISBN 978-1-63188-968-4 (hosted ebook)
  1. Pattern perception--Juvenile literature. 2. Food--Juvenile literature. I. Title.

BF294.F453 2015
152.14'23--dc23

2014029999

Cherry Lake Publishing would like to acknowledge the work of The Partnership for 21st Century Skills. Please visit *www.p21.org* for more information.

Printed in the United States of America
Corporate Graphics Inc.
December 2014

TABLE OF CONTENTS

What Do You See?

What food do you see in this honeycomb?

Patterns

Did you know many foods show patterns? Patterns are things that **repeat**. Shapes repeat in this **honeycomb**.

Patterns have **cores**. Cores repeat twice or more. They repeat in **order**.

James lines up fruit in a pattern. The core is apple, orange.

What Do You See?

Where do you see another pattern
in this photo?

Treats

Grant's cookies are stacked chocolate, vanilla. This is an AB pattern.

Letters help us see cores. Quinn's candy is red and white. Call red A. Call white B. The core is AB.

Colors repeat in Kat's jar of gumballs. But they do not repeat in order. They do *not* show a pattern.

What's Next?

Kira eats kabobs for dinner. They show an AB pattern of chicken, tomato. **Predict** what's next after tomato!

What Do You See?

How many peppers do you see?

These peppers show a color pattern. Use letters to find the core.

Kade's birthday cake has ice cream cones! Give each colored cone a letter. What is the core?

What is your favorite patterned food?

21

Find Out More

BOOK

McGrath, Barbara Barbieri. *Teddy Bear Patterns*. Watertown, MA: Charlesbridge, 2013.

WEB SITE

Pattern Matcher—PBS Parents
www.pbs.org/parents/education/math/games/preschool-kindergarten/pattern-matcher/
Play a game completing food, animal, and people patterns.

Glossary

cores (KORZ) the smallest repeating parts of a pattern

honeycomb (HUHN-ee-kohm) rows of wax cells made inside a hive by bees

order (OR-dur) set in a repeating way

predict (pree-DIKT) to say what will come next or in the future

repeat (ri-PEET) to appear or happen again and again

Home and School Connection

Use this list of words from the book to help your child become a better reader. Word games and writing activities can help beginning readers reinforce literacy skills.

apple	eats	letters	red
birthday	favorite	lines	repeat
cake	find	many	shapes
candy	foods	more	show
chicken	fruit	next	stacked
chocolate	gumballs	orange	things
colors	honeycomb	order	tomato
cones	ice cream	patterned	treats
cookies	jar	patterns	twice
cores	kabobs	peppers	vanilla
dinner	know	predict	white

What Do You See?

What Do You See? is a feature paired with select photos in this book. It encourages young readers to interact with visual images in order to build the ability to integrate content in various media formats.

You can help your child further evaluate photos in this book with additional activities. Look at the images in the book without the What Do You See? feature. Ask your child to describe one detail in each image, such as a color, activity, or setting.

Index

About the Author

Rebecca Felix is a writer and editor from Saint Paul, Minnesota. She enjoys many foods that show patterns. Striped candy is her favorite patterned food!